Simply Speaking Inspirations

A compilation of inspirational messages

SHERRY D. BAILEY

authorHOUSE®

AuthorHouse™ LLC
1663 Liberty Drive
Bloomington, IN 47403
www.authorhouse.com
Phone: 1-800-839-8640

Published by AuthorHouse   05/19/2014

ISBN: 978-1-4969-1327-2 (sc)
ISBN: 978-1-4969-1325-8 (e)

Table of Contents

Are You Going with the Flow?

Have you ever thrown a stick into the water and watched it float down stream? If so, perhaps you noticed the current caused the stick to uncontrollably swirl around? You noticed how it carried the stick in a direction that caused it to become tangled in debris? Or maybe you noticed how it tossed the stick back and forth against protruding rocks in the stream. Now imagine yourself as the stick.

Take a moment to look back over your life. Can you remember a time when there was no direction in your life? Can you remember when much like the stick you had no control of where your life was heading? Of course you have. The truth is we all have. We were going with the FLOW. In other words, we were **F**reely **L**iving **O**ur **O**wn **W**ill.

Many of you reading this are still freely living your own will. And yet you sense within your spirit that you are out of sync with God's direction and plan for your life. You are not alone. Whether you are a seasoned Christian or a babe in Christ, we all have a tendency to lift up our anchor (the Word and Will of God) and let life's circumstances carry us wherever it pleases. It can be a hard road getting back; but thanks be to God we can get back. The following suggestions are three steps to help you do just that. You can:

- Recognize God in the flow. When you recognize God in the flow your perspective changes and you begin to realize that things are not as dismal as you originally

1

thought. You may glance at your problem, but your mind, body and soul gazes in reverence at God. You are in awe because you know that He is able to take life's ups and downs and divinely direct them for your good.

- Relinquish control. The very word "relinquish" means to give up or surrender. When you relinquish control, you are saying, "not my will Lord, but thou will be done." You are telling God that you want what He wants for your life. You are willing to let go of those things that keep you from drawing closer to Him. And you recognize His ability to change the direction of your life. Zechariah 4:6 states, "*not by might, nor by power, but by my spirit says the Lord Almighty.*" More times than not we need to relinquish our control and let God handle it.

- Relate to God in the water. Relating to God in the water is knowing that He is divinely orchestrating your every move and you are willing to let Him. You're not fighting against him, but flowing with Him. Relating to God in the water cleanses you. Hebrews 10:22 states, "*let us draw near to God with a sincere heart in full assurance of faith, having our hearts sprinkled to cleanse us from a guilty conscience having our bodies washed in pure water.*" Relating to God in the water is assimilating to your natural environment. It is knowing that you're in the right place at the right time. And God is the conductor not the caboose of your life. So stay in position and allow God to orchestrate your next move.

If we only recognize God in the flow, relinquish control and relate to Him, he will infuse us with his living water. In that living water there is God's perfect flow of timing, his perfect flow of perfection and his perfect flow of righteousness. If you want this living water all you have to do is ask. God will freely pour into you and you will witness His abundant FLOW. Why not let him?

Do You Fear the Lord?

It's a simple question. Do you fear the Lord? Don't answer too quickly. You may be deceived. I would like to believe that as Christians we do fear the Lord. But what does it really mean to fear the Lord? In my meditation time I was reading Psalm 19:9, which states, "*The fear of the Lord is pure, enduring forever. The ordinances of the Lord are sure and altogether righteous.*" In my footnotes, I read, the fear of the Lord is an Old Testament expression meaning "reverential trust" including the hatred of evil. So that tells me that if I hate evil then I fear the Lord, right? Wrong. I can hear about a horrific crime on the news and say that I hate what happened, but that doesn't mean I fear the Lord.

I believe fearing the Lord is putting absolute trust and confidence in God. It is knowing that He will provide for all of your needs. It is knowing that he will answer every cry for help. It's knowing that he will see you through every situation; big or small. I believe fearing the Lord means that even when you can't see Jesus working in your life; he is still there. And when there's no evidence of his work; you know intrinsically that He is there interceding on your behalf to the Father. And as the Master of the Universe; he will make everything alright. That is fearing the Lord.

And it also means that you don't just behave in any kind of way. If you are a child of the King you are a called out people. According to 1 Peter 2:9 we are, "*a holy nation; a royal priesthood; a people belonging to God.*" When you fear the Lord—you're in a blood covenant relationship that you take very seriously thus; you do everything in your power not to destroy that trust. Fearing the Lord means that you know there are repercussions to your actions. And you don't want to suffer the consequences of disobedience. Therefore you strive and thrive to please your partner—Jesus, right? After all he sealed you with his redemptive blood. Nothing can penetrate that bond. And nobody else can do that, but Jesus!

My meditation time revealed "*the fear of the Lord is the beginning of knowledge, but fools despise wisdom and discipline*" according to Proverbs 1:7. So here again it seems reasonable to conclude that fearing the Lord is a good thing. After all I don't want to be known as a "fool," nor do you I hope. And when I continued to read, in my footnotes it said, a "fool" in scripture refers to someone who is arrogant and self-sufficient; and one who orders his life as if there was no God. (Luke 12:16-21). Thanks goodness, that's not you or me. But there is a good example of a fool in scripture. It is the behavior of the rich man. He was not mentally deficient, but he was a fool because he thought his soul could live on the things stored up in his barn. However, he did not give any thought to his eternal well-being. Who wants to leave a legacy of being known as a fool? Not me. Do you? So it would behoove us to live in the fear of the Lord because that is profitable. And it's much better to be remembered as intelligent or witty rather than being labeled as a "fool."

Another scripture that demands your attention is Proverbs 19:28, it states, "*penalties are prepared for mockers, and beatings for the backs of fools*." Well now, how much clearer of a picture do I have to paint for you? Isn't it obvious that fools are simply that—ignorant to the unmitigated awe of God's goodness. Shouldn't there be something in your psyche that bears witness to his wondrous working power, right now!

Proverbs 14:1 states, "*the wise woman builds her house, but with her own hands the foolish [woman] tears hers down.*" That goes for men too. You have a choice. You can choose to seek God's guidance and gain wisdom or you can choose to be a fool. Your demise will be on your own hands if you choose the latter. When I read this scripture I was indignant. I was livid. I was convicted because I realize that I had been guilty of tearing down my own house. But now I know better. I know the truth. God's Word says, "*if you hold to my teaching, you are my disciples. Then you know the truth and the truth sets you free.*" (John 8:31b-32). I've been set free from my condemnation and convictions. You can be too. I am so glad I know Jesus and he knows me intimately. We all have a choice to tear down or build up. It's up to you. Be determined to live righteously and watch your rate of return.

In my deeper study of fearing the Lord I discovered another scripture. In Proverbs 2:1-5, it states, "*My son, if you accept my words and store up my commands within you, turning your ear to wisdom and applying your heart to understanding, and if you call out for insight and cry aloud for understanding, and if you look for it as for hidden treasure then you will understand the fear of the Lord and find the knowledge of God.*" So it will be safe to surmise that the fear of the Lord is like a seed in your soul. It is no good to you until you plant it deep into the pit of your soul. As time passes you will notice that you have more wherewithal and stamina than you thought. When the storms of life come raging your response will be fortified with faith. It will not destroy you. On the contrary, your spirit will bear witness to the fruit that has been germinating inside of you.

I fear him because he is my Savior, my Rock, and my Redeemer. I cannot tell it all, but I can tell some of it. Fearing the Lord is the place to be. It's the place for me. What about you?

Another thought-provoking scripture that stopped me in my tracks was Job 28:28 which states, "***the fear of the Lord— that is wisdom, and to shun evil is understanding.***" Even Job searched for wisdom from God. In his pursuit he discovered that "fearing the Lord" meant he had to endure: heartache, trouble, abandonment and physical ailment and more. Even we, as children of God experience a monsoon of trouble and pain, but it is through those wilderness experiences that we understand "fearing the Lord." It is a journey that ushers us to our destination with fear and trembling because we respect (reverence) the King of Kings! He made us. He molded us. He created us to be like him. We are not exempt from pain or trouble. Instead it is during those times of trouble that we should "trust" the Lord even more. We are preprogrammed to experience the grittiness of life. But that shouldn't make us give up; rather it should provoke us to "look up!" A heavenly perspective is the direction our attitude should point to.

The final scripture I wish to share is, "***a wise man fears the Lord and shuns evil, but a fool is hotheaded and reckless.***" (Proverbs 14:16). The question remains, do you fear the Lord? I know I do.

Ecstasy is For You!

Ecstasy is an overwhelming feeling of happiness or great excitement! That is what we long to feel. Am I right? It is a state of utter bliss. It is a non-stop feeling of joy. I know some of you may think of the drug "ecstasy" but I'm not talking about a drug. No. I am talking about a feeling that surpasses euphoria or happiness. I am talking about a feeling of unmistakable transcendence.

What is that you say? You don't know what transcendence is? I will be happy to share my definition of transcendence. It is a state of being transported to another place. In other words, it's like having an out of body experience. To make it a little clearer, I would have to say that it is the opposite of suffering. You get it? Yes. It is a sensation of unparalleled joy. And there are no side effects like the drug "ecstasy" may give you. Rather it is sustained happiness. Oh my, what a feeling. I'm sure as humans it is something we desire to capture and keep. However few of us ever experience it. And that is a shame. But it doesn't have to remain that way. God intends for us to experience ecstasy. Do you believe that? If you don't believe me, give me a chance to convince you.

No one starts out in life wanting to suffer. We all desire to avoid suffering at any cost. But life is just not life without it. Pinpointing hardships in our lives usually arrive us at place of questioning our decision-making. We often ask the question, "Why me? or Why now? Or we may simply ask, "Why?" As children we were taught not to question God's divine sovereignty or his divine will. But I am not sure if I agree with that notion. Nevertheless, we must continue to live. I believe the more important question to ask is how. How do we live? And who are we living for? How we live has a direct effect on how much ecstasy we experience. Who we are living for has a direct effect on how much ecstasy we experience. If we are living for God than our conduct should align with our Father's will. We experience ecstasy as a result of our reverence to him. Ecstasy is an outgrowth of our obedience to the Master. Remember the last time you had a huge problem and God intervened and solved it? That was ecstasy!

Remember when your bill was late and you didn't have the funds to pay it, but miraculously God stepped in and made everything alright? That was ecstasy! Remember when you could have lost your temper and sent someone to the hospital, but God kept you from snapping? That was ecstasy! Have you forgotten when he taught you in his word, "I came to give you life and life more abundantly." (John 10:10). That's ecstasy baby! Don't you know when God gives you joy—it's like nothing in the world. When you have ecstasy you have transcended joy and entered in the presence of the Almighty!

In my research study of "suffering," I discovered the meaning of suffering is to endure hardship; which literally means to "suffer together with someone." You mean we are not alone when we suffer? It sounds incredible, right? But it's not. You are never alone when you suffer. I know the devil would like for you to believe otherwise. But it's true. You are not alone. God is with you. The bible tells us God, "will never leave you, never will (HE) forsake you." (Heb 13:5b). So we can count on God to keep his promise. God is the only person who CANNOT lie. As a matter of fact we are to look forward to suffering. And when we do; we are to rejoice! In other words, we are to experience ecstasy. It says so in 1 Peter 4:12, "don't think something strange is happening to you, but rejoice that you participate in the sufferings of Christ; so that you may be overjoyed when his glory is revealed." That's ecstasy baby!

We really need to get it! Ecstasy goes beyond joy! In order to experience joy you have go through suffering. It is a mandate. It is unavoidable. It is a mark of a Christian. And not only that, but God says it's according to his will. So stop your crying and whining and start serving the Master. Why? Because Daddy said so, "those who suffer (according to God's will) should commit themselves to their faithful Creator and continue to do good." (1 Peter 4:19) Now, how about those apples? If you think you have been through a lot, stop for a moment; evaluate your life in comparison to Christ and then get your head back on track.

I know there are times when you think your suffering has hit its limit. And you are ready to lash out in anger, desperation or retaliation, but don't do it for the sake of the Son. Jesus is your advocate. He defeated Satan, surely he can handle your situation. So if we suffer together with someone, we should recognize that that someone is Jesus. He will not let us down. He is always around. And he wants and desires for you to experience ecstasy baby!

Follow Your First Love

In recent months God has led me on a spiritual fast. This fast was unlike any I've done before. I heard the Lord say, "eat no meat, or unclean thing that sheds blood—nothing dead shall enter your temple. You are to be a *"channel"* of blessings, as Abraham." I don't know what it all meant. And I didn't understand it, but I choose to follow my first love—My Lord. Why because he loves me, he told me so. (John 3:16). If any of you have ever been in a place where you didn't understand what was happening in your life—but you continued to follow and trust God—that's good. That is exactly where God wants you—He wants you depending on him alone. It seems things are being uprooted all around me; my job is shaky, my relationship with my church members is sporadic; and my situation at home seems uncertain. But to God be the glory!

Have you ever been there? Well if you haven't hold on, it's coming. Like I said in recent months God has declared a spiritual fast for me. But I really don't consider it a "fast" but more of a lifestyle. Only God knows for sure. I really feel like its preparation season for where's he is taking me. Don't ever doubt God's power or his sovereignty. He can do whatever he wants. He desires for us to trust him in everything; even the minute details of our lives. Therefore, our first love should be to God. Without him nothing you do in life makes sense.

Since I've been on this journey I had things happen that signify that only God is in control. Praise Jesus! For example,

I sat next to a man I didn't know at a Conference and the Holy Spirit said, "write this on the paper and hand it to him." I was obedient. After the man read it—he touched me on the shoulder with tears in his eyes and asked me, "how did you know?" I replied, "I didn't. The Holy Spirit did and I only did what he told me. And that's exactly what you must do." The words I wrote to him where, "you have a goal in your heart you want to do it, God says get to work doing it." The man shook my hand and thanked me. I thanked God.

On that same day God allowed me to encounter a dear sister in the faith. I spent time listening to her share her heart. And from that occasion a stronger bond of friendship developed. It was God. Numerous events similar to those have taken place as well. I attribute them all to God's goodness. You see when you are faithful and obedient with the small things in life God will make you ruler of much (Matt 25:21). But he needs to find us faithful. Many times we are willing to do the big things in life for notoriety and fame, however; God is asking us, "will you walk across the street and share your faith with the neighbor?"(today). The things that are most important to God are the things he will test you in to see if you're really his—do you exemplify his character?

The proof is in the pudding. When we get serious about our journey with God and do as he has commanded we will see miraculous and powerful things happen in the lives of others and ourselves. But remember he desires your obedience (1 Sam 15:22).—Will you follow your first love?

Fall Spiritual Season of Life

We are going to talk about three distinct women who epitomize being subjected, dejected, rejected and neglected. And I'm sure their story it not unlike your own story. In invite you to journey with me down the road of grace as we peek in on the lives of three estranged women.

First we have the woman with the lascivious spirit; better known to us as a whore. You know who she is—you were probably her sometime in your own spiritual walk. A whore is any single or married woman who practices unlawful sexual indulgence; whether for gain or for lust. (unlawful sex is having sex outside of the marriage covenant. Let's look in Luke 7:36-39; and Luke 7:44-50 and unpack what we read. When we read the scripture, we notice that this sister heard about Jesus going to visit Brother Simon's house. And she decided that she would drop by. In the proceeding verses you will notice that this woman was:

- Deliberate
- Decisive and
- Determined

She was deliberate about where she was going because she wasn't invited to the dinner party; she just showed up. She was decisive about her entrance into the house because she could've been overcome by ridicule and condemnation by the other men and disciples sitting there but she didn't flint—she pursued her Master with decisiveness. And not only was she deliberate about where she was going, decisive about what she was going to do; but the text says she brought an alabaster jar with her, because she was determined to get to Jesus. In her mind she had no other recourse but to pursue Jesus regardless of her condition and regardless of her social position in life. She made up in her mind that she had to touch Jesus. Not only did she touch Jesus—but she used her hair to brush and anoint Jesus' feet. As she carefully and delicately kissed Jesus' feet she methodically poured oil on his feet. Some of us are just like this woman. We want to touch Jesus. And we will do anything to get close enough to feel his warm embrace. Are you that determined, that decisive and that deliberate woman?

Secondly, we have another sister in the word we want to look in on. She is a woman with issues. Let's look at her story. Turn to Luke 8:43-48. Here we see a sister better known to us as a "bitch." I know if I had been bleeding for 12 long—long—long years without any relief in sight; given all my money to the doctors and still kept seeing blood I would be a bitch too. The scripture says she had been suffering for 12, count them 12 long years with this issue. I can relate to this sister because I was hemorrhaging a few months ago and it wasn't for 12 years; more like two to three weeks and I almost killed somebody. But to God be the glory. Amen. One can consider that this woman was not only suffering from an uncontrollable blood flow, but she had other issues as well. Some of us can relate to her with our own issues of lying, overeating, over spending; gossiping and the list can go on and on. No matter what the "issue" sister girl had a problem. Right? Not only was this sister suffering, but we can see from the text that she was:

- Destitute
- Desperate and
- Daring

This sister was on point when it came to going after what she wanted. Her desire was to touch Jesus. Not only did she want to touch Jesus, but she had to be healed. Sister was destitute because scripture says she had spent all of her money on physicians. All her money was gone. Therefore, she was destitute. When you're destitute rational thinking is not on your top priority list. This is evident by her disregard for the crowd. She was daring to take matters in her own hands. She showed that by pushing her way through the crowd. She tossed caution to the wind. Even though she could've been trampled to death by the crowd, her desperation ignited her to act. Sister demonstrated that desperate times called for desperate measures. Not only was she daring, but she was determined to get close to Jesus so that she could "touch" the hem of his garment. She had to touch H-I-M that was covered in H-E-M. I believe at some point in our own life we to can relate to this woman with our issues. Whether our issue is overspending, over eating or lying we too can get to Jesus if we're desperate enough; daring enough and determined enough to seek him out. Is that you?

Our final sister we're going to talk about is found in Luke 13:10-13. This woman is what I call a heifer. Why do I call her a heifer? I call her a heifer because heifers are known as being a young cow; or a full grown ox. They are also known for being "messy" by always throwing old stuff up in your face from your past; and they are usually resistant to authority and very stubborn. Heifers are usually called "beast of burden." It was obvious this woman was a product of her environment. She had been burdened down so much that it showed up in her physical body. The text said she was bent over. Does that sound like anybody you know?

The woman we see in the text had been stricken with a condemning spirit. She probably had been beaten; bruised, and broken in spirit by so many folks that she was at a point of despondency. And rightly so, the scripture said she had been "bent over" for 18 years! Consider 18 years of being called out of your name; being laughed at; belittled and demeaned until finally she came to a place of being depleted. It was probably because of the abuse and neglect that she experienced that she employed her only coping mechanism for dealing with her pain—which was depression. Some of you can probably relate to this sister. She was:

- Despondent
- Depleted
- Distraught
- Desensitized
- Deranged
- Delusional and
- Deceived

Sister was despondent because she sat with the crowd hoping to blend in; not wanting anyone to notice her; especially not Jesus. She wasn't looking for Jesus. She saw Jesus and didn't bid him over. She was despondent because she was fit to be tired of drumming up false hope of being set free from her infirmity. Sister girl was depleted spiritually because she had lost her joy. Her praises had turn into whims of pitiful me and sorrowful sighs of "why me," and faint grunts of "I'm disgusting." Sister was distraught because she didn't look like the other women in the village. She didn't have a fine frame and luxurious long hair flowing down her back or a beautiful face that men could adore. She was messed up from the floor up because she couldn't straighten up. She was desensitized to her surroundings because it didn't bother her that she was a lame woman walking; albeit slowly and malignantly.

She was still walking. She was deranged because how are you going to sit up in church in the presence of power and not be changed? Some of us here are still doing that. She was delusional because when you know you're sick and you don't cry out for help; it's because you've been deceived. The enemy had deceived her into thinking that she wasn't going to get any better. She was in the presence of power and couldn't respond. She was in the midst of the crowd probably trying to pretend that there was nothing wrong with her, but the text says she had an "infirmity." In biblical times an infirmity could mean three (3) things: 1) impurity meaning "menstruation" or 2) deformity; or possibly 3) disability. This woman was spiritually depleted, mentally deranged and physically deformed. Her infirmity was tripled-fold. But the good news for this sister is that she came to the right church that day. She encountered the God-head Trinity:

Jesus saw her. And when Jesus saw her instantly she was delivered. She didn't have to ask Jesus if he would heal her. The woman's spirit testified to Jesus on her behalf. (Romans 8:26). When Jesus declared she was healed; she was straight.

When Jesus decreed her wholeness; she danced.

When Jesus denounced the enemy's hold on her; she praised God.

The text says this woman praised God. I thought to myself how do you praise God without making some noise? I truly believe the moment this woman was delivered she not only danced, but she shouted, she sung and she couldn't help herself but tell others what Jesus had done for her. Unlike the other two sisters in Luke who initiated the touch to Jesus and Jesus told them their faith made them whole and to go in peace. One thing that separated this woman from the other two is that she didn't keep her deliverance to herself. She didn't go in peace; instead she went telling everybody about a man. She went praising and singing of the good news of God. She went sharing the good news of how God delivered her from all of her issues; from all of her infirmities; from all of her mental illnesses and from all of her physical sickness. That is something to shout about!

The life application for us is when you find yourself falling God wants you to:

- Shout

- Sing and

- Share

Shout how the Savior brought you out! Sing of his goodness! And share your testimony of God's wonder working power with others. Share your love of him with the world. Share the dramatic change in your life since Jesus set you free. Share your heart with a lonely person. Share your joy and sorrow expecting a better tomorrow. Jesus is the cure for all of our hurt and pain. Allow him to manifest miracles in your life. Trust him to catapult your Fall Season into Spring. The fruit of his Spirit always produces more than enough.

God Has Spoken

Yes! God has spoken! He has declared, "You are my witnesses, declares the Lord and my servant whom I have chosen, so that you may know and believe in me and understand that I am he." (Isaiah 43:10). Those words and more are what God gave me when he demonstrated a divine impartation through a beloved sister; Rachel Banks. It happened on Sunday, July 23, 2006. I had a divine encounter with the Master.

And yes it was real and prophetic. On Monday, July 24, 2006, I asked God, "did you call me to preach . . . yes or no?" He answered with Isaiah 43:10 and he confirmed it with Isaiah 43:15. Then he reiterated in Isaiah 43:18.

I LOVE GOD. He is so amazing! He is incredible! He is outstanding! There is no one who can compare to our AWESOME GOD! Let me fully delineate what he said in Isaiah 43:15, so that you can receive the full magnitude of this word; he said, "I am the Lord, your Holy One, Israel's Creator, your King!" And if that wasn't clear enough for you he reiterated his purpose in Isaiah 43:18 by stating, "Forget the former things; do not dwell on the past. See I am doing a new thing! Now it springs up; do you not perceive it? I'm making a way in the desert and streams in the wasteland." Holler somebody if you hear me? I'm just sharing what God said to me. Permit me to be transparent. I am crystal clear on my purpose now! God has given me his mandate. I accept it wholeheartedly and willingly. I recognize that this is the most ultimate privilege and honor. I have been chosen by God to preach and teach his gospel. I joyfully accept and submit to his sovereignty. Do it God. All I can say is "yes" and "Amen." HALLELJUAH!!!! Ain't nobody BAD like you JESUS! I mean that in a good way—you understand.

There's not much else to say. But watch, work and pray. Watch for God to work in my life and your life. Continue to pray that God has his way because he will; regardless if you pray or not. And continue to watch for marvelous manifestations of God's presence in your life. I want to thank my family, friends and church for supporting me. And I pray that you will continue to support me. I especially want to sincerely thank my husband, Rev. Cedric L. B. Mitchell, III for accepting God's call on my life and embracing it. That was no easy task. But to God be the glory. I thank him for his love and support. (*pseudo support, not actual it was for public image only. Read my book, "A Kept Woman" and you will understand*).

My future columns will acknowledge and underscore my new calling as a "minister." I pray those of you who read this would continue to pray for my family, and me, as I will for you. My desire is that you pray unceasingly for God to reveal your purpose. I pray that you will walk in your anointed purpose and calling. And remember to continue to read, study and pray. Do as Jeremiah said in chapter 33 verse 3, "Call to me and I will answer you and tell you great and unsearchable things you do not know."

Holler If You Hear Me

God is teaching me 1 Peter 4:10-11 and Ephesians 4:29. Basically in 1 Peter 4:10 it states, "*we should use our gift God gave us to serve others.*" We should do it faithfully so that others are being served God's grace. Simply put, grace is receiving what you don't deserve. Serving others is our spiritual act of worship. In verse 11 of 1 Peter it states if we speak we should, "*speak as one speaking the very words of God.*" The cross reference scripture is in Ephesians 4:29, which states, "*do not let any unwholesome talk come out of your mouth, but only what is helpful for building others up according to their needs. This will benefit those who listen.*" WOW!

The whole idea of watching what you say and speaking the very words of God is not an easy task. As a matter of fact is very foreboding—especially when you know your own weaknesses. When you know what your gift is (that God reveals), and you use it to serve others, God will reward your faithfulness and obedience. I know that I would love to be able to say that I weigh each word that comes out of my mouth, but that wouldn't be the truth. It is a daily task that I have to work on. Just like it is hard to speak the very words of God as if I were God himself—it's a work in progress. We can plot out an upward target and if we miss the mark we can persevere. Striding harder will get us closer to the mark, next time.

Recently I accepted an invitation to speak at a Women's Retreat. I cannot tell you how painstakingly time consuming it was to prepare. My desire was to speak eloquently, concisely and simply; so that I could be understood, while at the same time be cognizant of the fact that I should speak the very words of God. I pray that it was accomplished. I really don't believe we weigh our words until we see them in print. It is then that we can fully understand the magnitude of 1 Peter 4:11.

One of the speaking topics I share with others is entitled, "Off the Edge, No Turning Back." I feel like that right now, because I have taken this huge leap of faith. And I must plot ahead. I cannot turn back. Now that Simply Speaking Consulting© is worldwide people expect for you to deliver on the service you promote. It is not easy getting there. But I know with God's help, I can do all things. If you find yourself in a similar situation where you feel you cannot turn back, my advice to you is to: 1) holler out; 2) hold on; and 3) heed God's voice. First, you want to holler. It does something to your body. It's a release. And you actually feel better. Most of the time hollering is an automatic response when you're in trouble or when pressure has taken its toil. We tend to holler when we're holding on to frustration. When you holler it signals an emergency call to Heaven and Jesus is ready to respond. After you holler you should hold on to your senses to watch and see what's about to happen next. You do know your Father is a Keeper. By holding on—you're making a conscious decision to wait on God. Holding signifies anticipation. Anticipation signifies expectation. Expectation signifies the manifestation of God to work things out. Just hold on, stay strong and watch the Master work it out.

Finally, you want to heed God's voice (His Word) because it is perfect and right. And you never go wrong when you use the basic instruction manual for life—the bible. When you heed God's voice He promises that He will never leave nor forsake you. When we diligently seek after him, Jeremiah says, "*you will find him (me) when you seek me with all your heart*." (Jer 29:13).

So again, weigh your words carefully and seek God for guidance. He is always present and he dispenses the best advice. Have you hollered today?

I Made It Over

It is a new year! PRAISE THE LORD! Thank God we made it over! How are you going to live the next 12 months of your life? How about living like you are ready to die? That doesn't sound appealing. No doubt, but it's a reality. We all have to go that way some day. But the good news is—it's not over at the grave. We, who are Christians, have the glorious privilege of living forever in eternity! That's where you want to be. It would do us well to get busy living life today like we're going to die tomorrow. You don't know what tomorrow is going to bring, but we do know the King of Kings! And he is the Master of everything.

I had a vision of my life's end; thinking of the people and what they would say. Then, I thought it doesn't matter. What matters most is how I lived. If we were afforded the privilege of seeing a snapshot of our life's end; knowing when and where it terminated would you get busy doing the things you always talked about, but never had the time to do? Well, why not start today? You can give your best in service, your best in love to your family; your best in working; your best in living. Simply give your best in whatever God calls you to do. Then you can go to eternity knowing that God is pleased and your living was not in vain.

In Ezekiel 24:18, I read, "*so I spoke to the people in the morning and in the evening m wife died. The next morning I did as I had been commanded.*" How is it this prophet of old lost his wife, prophesized to the people, carried the mantle of God and yet he did not take time out to grieve? What's up with that? As a matter of fact, Ezekiel was a dumb mute until God gave him utterance. (Ezekiel 3:26). Just as it was with Ezekiel, so it is with you and I. We must obey when God says, "son or daughter" do as I say. Let's not miss our opportunity to change the world for God. The Lord is the only One whose opinions matters. We should strive each day to live like it was our last. In doing so, you can rest assured that you won't have any regrets.

Ezekiel's purpose was to prophesy to the people. He warned them against impending destruction. That destruction was in the form of idolatry, lewdness and prostitution. He warned them against every abomination imaginable—but they refused to listen. As a result, God destroyed the "delight of their eyes." (Ezk 24:15)—their Temple. In the midst of this destruction, God told Ezekiel not to mourn or shed a tear; instead groan quietly. How do you groan quietly? Then he told him, "keep your turban and sandals on your feet; do not cover the lower part of your face or eat customary food of mourners." (v.17). Then on top of all that, God snatched his wife from the scene (v.18) and Ezekiel was not allowed to cry, shout or shed a tear. He didn't even make funeral arrangements. Instead Ezekiel was to be a sign (v.24) for all of Israel to see the sovereignty of the Lord! Would you have such a testimony?

In this year of our Lord, strive to be your best as never before. Don't dig up pains from the past; don't lament about short-comings of the present and don't sift through uncertainties of the future; instead courageously cling to the Master's Hand.

Let him lead, guide and direct your paths. In the end, nothing else matters—only that you walked with the Lord and you did as he had commanded. Amen.

Imitator or Perpetrator — Which are You?

Imitate means to mimic or to act like someone. Perpetrate means to commit or be guilty of. They both sound the same, but as far as their definition, they are diametrically different. How? Easy. Imitate is to be like. Perpetrate is to be "guilty" of doing something *illegally*. In other words, you are guilty of not being authentic, genuine or real Christian. Does that mean being a fake Christian is illegal? Yes it is. God said it was. Knowing the right thing to do and not doing it is a sin. That's illegal in God's eyes. The question is, which one are you? There are some people in the body of Christ who pretend to love you when in their hearts they really don't. These people are perpetrators. They are guilty of not being genuine. We should be very careful of those people.

What perpetrators do is pretend. They shake. They fake. They pretend to have an authentic relationship with you. And they pretend to celebrate with you when they see you coming, but the moment your back is turned they stab you. You see perpetrators keep mess stirred up. They love to be at the meeting when controversy arises or if major decisions have to be made to block progress. They would rather see you stuck like Chuck in the middle of muck rather than help to make God's kingdom grow. What's even worse is that perpetrators say, "I'm blessed," "praise the Lord" or even, "Amen," but in their own personal life they don't have any power over their circumstances. Their prayer life is full of repetition over the same issues because they are afraid to grow spiritually and let God use them for his service. What kind of life is that? It really gets on my nerve when I hear perpetrators say, "I'm blessed in the Lord, sister." Or they say, "I'm highly favored walking in abundance," but then they turn around and ask you for money or quiz you about your blessings, what's up? Haven't you been praying for a breakthrough? If they really have power it would evident, not a contradiction. I hope you don't fall in that category.

Imitators on the other hand, have real power. They are full of encouragement, enthusiasm and vigor! Most of them are eager to help you; pray for you and serve in any capacity. And they do it without asking you a lot of questions. The Word of God states, "*be imitators of God as dearly loved children, live a life of love as Jesus gave himself up for us as a fragrant offering and sacrifice to God.*" (Galatians 5:2). Try living your life without comparing it to others.

It is our duty to love one another and be like Jesus. He gave himself up for us. The least we can do is give our self back to him. (consider all that he has done for us). If I can't convince you to be an imitator—perhaps God's Word can. As I was studying the scriptures, God said to be an imitator of me, you must be like me. Well, how do I act like Jesus? Simple, ask yourself what did Jesus do? He loved. He forgave. He showed mercy. He blessed. He spoke life. He rebuked. He reproved. He did everything good for us that we were not able to do on our own. If we're going to imitate Christ, we must behave in a manner that is Christ-like. That means we have to be led by the Spirit and not by our flesh. Since we are his children, we should act like our Father. When your children misbehave don't you question who they belong to? Sometimes, we go so far as to tell them, "I don't know whose child you are—because no child of mine would act like that." How do you think God feels about you when we don't behave in a way that is becoming to him? God calls us to imitate his character, his likeness and his image.

Further study revealed God calls us to live a life of love. He even tells us to speak to each other in love. Ephesians 4:15 states, "*speaking the truth in love, we will in all things grow up into him who is the Head, that is Christ.*" Wouldn't it be a shame if your child never grew up? If our children remained children all their life—there would be something wrong, right? Of course it would; because that is not normal progression. So it is with our spiritual life. If we're not growing spiritually, attaining more knowledge, gaining more power and growing in our faith; then we should question our faith. What is it you're doing? In order for a child to reach his full potential he has to grow up. So should we. God calls us to live a life of love. By living we are growing and hopefully maturing spiritually in the process.

Who of you would plant a fruit tree one day and the next day pull it up because it didn't have any fruit? That's not reasonable or realistic. We have to give the tree time to grow so that it can produce fruit. That is what God is saying to you. Plant your roots deep into the Word of God and allow him to grow you spiritually. It will take some time, but the results will be beneficial for you and others.

Being imitators of Christ requires us to give. We give ourselves in service. We give to others. We give by working.

We give in response to Jesus' ultimate sacrifice on the Cross. We give because he gave. The more we give, the more we should live to please God. Jesus gave himself to the world, so that none would be lost. How much more should we want to live, forgive and give our love to others. It would help them to heal and receive the greatest gift of love—Jesus! As imitators of God, we must give. God's word's says, "*give, and it shall be given unto you; a good measure, pressed down, and shaken together, and running over shall men give into your bosom.*" (Luke 6:38). The more you give of yourself the more God will give unto you.

Jesus became the peace offering in our stead to please God. He was and is the efficacious propitiation. Literally translated it means He (Jesus) was the most "effective good will offering" to God for our sins. Since Jesus gave so should we. Give and watch God work. Remember what Paul said in Romans 4:21, "*being full persuaded that what he had promised, he is well able to perform.*" I consider that as the undisputed, irrevocable word of truth. My God cannot lie nor change his mind.

A sure fire way to test to see if you're an imitator or perpetrator is to watch the results of what happens when you're tempted. The character trait that dominates will reveal your answer. If you succumb to sin by giving in; then you're tempted. You may be a perpetrator. If you restrain from temptation then you're a true imitator. Go ahead, imitate him. I dare you. He is watching.

Intimacy With God

Intimacy with God . . . is knowing the Father and he knows you.

Intimacy with God . . . is going before his throne with all your concerns and issues and letting him direct you on what to do.

Intimacy with God is . . . facing your failure and shortcomings and allowing God to reshape and remold you.

Intimacy with God . . . is calling on him when blessings are flowing and not flowing in your life.

Intimacy with God . . . is offering up praises to His name simply because God's character demands it.

Intimacy with God . . . is serving God with a new spirit and a new heart.

Intimacy with God . . . is calling those things that be not as they are and walking in it.

Intimacy with God . . . is having the assurance that God can handle any problem, any situation, any crisis in your life when you're sincerely turn it over to him.

Intimacy with God is . . . caring more about doing his will than yours.

Intimacy with God . . . calls you to think of others more highly than yourself.

Intimacy with God . . . allows you access to God's abundance whether it's his peace, his joy; his love; his long-suffering, his mercy, his grace, his forgiveness, his sovereignty, his presence, his power, his Spirit or his Son and get preferential treatment.

Intimacy with God . . . guarantees you a closer walk with God. It assures you top priority when you call on him.

Intimacy with God . . . allows you to serve God not out of your own capacity but out of His.

Intimacy with God . . . places God's power in your personal hand and at your fingertips.

Intimacy with God . . . demands a stronger prayer life thus a stronger walk.

Intimacy with God . . . causes you to care more about spiritual matters than worldly things.

Intimacy with God . . . will allow you to pray for your enemies and love them that despitefully use you.

Intimacy with God . . . will cause you to turn from sinning.

Intimacy with God . . . will give you peace that passes all understanding.

Intimacy with God . . . will make your enemies your footstool.

Intimacy with God . . . will call you out of your comfort zone.

Intimacy with God . . . will direct your paths and make your way straight.

Intimacy with God . . . is constantly renewing your mind and growing in the grace and knowledge of God.

Intimacy with God . . . is changing your direction in life as God dictates where he wants you to go.

Intimacy with God . . . is knowing the Father, the Son, and the Holy Spirit personally and they are permanent residents in your heart.

Intimacy with God . . . is doing what pleases God not man.

Intimacy with God . . . is waiting on God to move before you do.

Intimacy with God . . . is saying "no" to all the rest so that you can say "yes" to the best!

When was the last time you were intimate with God?

It's a Season of Change

Change doesn't come easily. It takes time. We desire change, but we seldom pursue it. In our quest for change we must realize **time** is on our side. Usually we fight against **time** thinking we don't have enough of it. However, that is quite the contrary. In a few short weeks, God has shown me how to "savor the moment." He has revealed that the season we're in is pivotal, precious and purposeful.

It's pivotal because in this season a "shift" will take place. God will "shift" something in your life that will change everything. Even the slightest alteration will reap great dividends when you embrace and recognize what's happening. During this pivotal time you will learn something significant about **who** you are in Christ.

This season of change is precious. It's precious because you can't get it back once you have used it. Change is precious because it's always meant to teach us a lesson. One considers something "precious" when we give it value. It is precious only to the beholder. If you consider life precious then you will live it more purposely and intentional. It will get better. I believe it is important for you to seek the "preciousness" of your life in order to discern what season you're in. Once you recognize what "season" you're in; then you can sensibly ascertain what move to make or what direction to take before making a fool of yourself.

This season of change is purposeful. It is purposeful because it is meant to enrich your life. It's purposeful in that **time** serves to make you a better person so that you can be a blessing to others. Remember **the more you give the more you live**. As children of God it would benefit us to know that God has divinely orchestrated every minute, every second, and every hour of our lives. We do ourselves displeasure when we deny it. In this season of change—learn to slow down, observe your surroundings, take in the scenery and savor the moment.

While recuperating from surgery God showed me a few things. These things helped me to see how I use my time. They were: take more time in the restroom, eat your food slower and talk slower. These three simple things have made a monumental impact in my daily life. I know more about myself and I'm in a better place to help someone else. Only God! When God shows you things about yourself—no one else can tell you differently. Thank you Jesus! You too can have it when your pursue intimacy with the Father. There is nothing like it! Conjure up the courage to approach God with all your issues and allow him to melt them away. Set your mind to sacrifice your most valuable treasure (your time) and see what God will do with it. Now give it to him. Not only will you be infinitely blessed—you will NOT be same. He will change your name from daughter or son to friend. Father Abraham is an example of this.

In James 2:23b it states, "**Abraham believed God and it was credited to him as righteousness, and he was called God's friend**." I don't know about you, but when God calls me "friend" that's a title I will gladly accept. Proverbs also solidifies this point in chapter 18 and verse 24, it states, "**a man of many companions may come to ruin, but there is a friend who sticks closer than a brother**." We know who that friend is—His name is JESUS! In this season of change, my prayer for you is to consider Jesus. And if you desire for him to call you friend; give him the gift of your time. It's the only gift you can't take back. The bible states, "**a gift opens the way for the giver and ushers him into the presence of the great.**" (Proverbs 18:16). Nothing is more important than your time with your Father.

A sermon I heard once was entitled, "It's Praying Time." The scripture reference was John 17:12. Here we have Jesus praying to his father. It is one of the most vivid pictures of the Father and Son. The preacher made a point in the sermon that our *power* is in prayer. He said we are no taller on our feet than we are on our knees. The *posture* of prayer is lifting up our eyes toward Heaven, the *focus* of our prayer is on the Father and the *place* of our prayer is in Heaven. Life is good if your perspective is good. Isn't it wonderful when you invest **your time** in the Son? And it's even better when the Son invests *your time* (you give Him) in the Father and the Father secures *your time* in the future—which is in Heaven. Jesus took time out to savor the moment with his Father . . . why don't you give it a try? It's time!

It's Ordination Time

In the Jewish tradition young boys have what they call a bar mitzvah; signifying a boy's coming of age or passage into manhood. In the Mexican American tradition a young girl's rites of passage is known as "quinceanera." However, in the African American culture no formal celebration is practiced, unless you would call a "coming out party" or a "debutante ball" likened to this type of event. The point I am getting at is this—we all have to grow up. At some point in your life you were "ordained" and sent out to live your life. Your parents taught you everything they knew and now it is up to you. We have all been equipped for service. What are you going to do? Another way of looking at this is by studying the scripture and reading how Moses prepared Aaron for the priesthood.

In Exodus 28 Moses received instruction from God on how to prepare his brother Aaron for the priesthood. In particular, verse 15 mentions the priest's breastplate and the items engraved in it. (precious stones, representing the 12 tribes of Israel). What really fascinates me was the mention of the Urim and Thummin. In verse 30 it states, "*also put the Urim and Thummin in the breastpiece so they may be over Aaron's heart, whenever he enters the presence of the Lord. Thus Aaron will always bear the means of making decisions for the Israelites over his heart before the Lord.*"

The two items that were placed over Aaron's heart are very significant. The Urim and Thummin represent "*light and perfection.*" Does that sound familiar? It should. Why? Because when you think of light and perfection you should think of Jesus, right? In my further research I discovered that these stones were used to ascertain the divine Will {of God} in some cases. (Num 27:21, Deut 33:8). The point that bears relevance here is that these precious stones were a part of the priestly garments Aaron and his sons wore when they were ordained as priests before God and the Israelites. In Leviticus 8:8, it states, **"He (Moses) placed the breastpiece on him (Aaron) and put the Urim and Thummin in the breastpiece."** The Urim and Thummin were used to bring illumination and truth of what God's divine will is. These two stones could cover any of the 12 stones to "illuminate" their beauty and brilliance. The Urim and Thummin were a "means" to bring more clarity to the situation.

It could be that in your own life you are seeking God for clarity or for his divine will. If so, he has given you the "means" to which to receive it. Remember *where* the two stones were placed? They were over the heart. The answer you are seeking from God is within you. It's in your heart! The reason you may not hear clearly could be that you are NOT actively seeking, pursuing and diligently asking God for HIS WILL, but your own. No matter how much you believe you are doing everything right, you must be honest with yourself and sincerely seek after God's Will.

In Moses' day the High Priest was anointed with oil. But animals had to be sacrificed before the oil could be poured. In other words, something had to die first. What habit, distraction or influence do you need to squash before you are ready to receive the oil of joy from the Lord? In God's word it states,

"God gives the spirit without limit." (John 3:34). That means God Spirit is limitless. He pours it out unto all who are willing to receive it. You have the power and direction you need if you only ask God with a sincere heart. He further states, *"your God has set you above your companions by anointing you with the oil of joy."* (Hebrews 1:9). So why not be joyous knowing that your day is coming?

There are two theories behind the Urim and Thummin. One theory is that they were used as an appendage that was detachable. And they could be cast like dice. By their fall; it revealed God's divine Will. This is a possible explanation, but there is no proof. The second theory is that the Urim and Thummin were used as a symbol. The High Priest arrayed himself in the ephod with the Urim and Thummin, which gave him the authority to obtain light and truth in order that he might seek counsel of Jehovah in a divinely appointed matter. Used as a symbol it was a means to an end. When the priest laid the matter before God in prayer, the answer dawned in his mind; therefore he humbly believed that he had the correct response. It sounds a lot like prayer, right? Isn't that what we do when we pray? Faith in God was the evidence of things not seen. This interpretation of the Urim and Thummin coincides with the spirituality and ritualism of the tabernacle.

The message for us to take away is that when we seek God with all of our heart the answer will come through inward illumination. Our ordination may not have happened with a mass convocation. We may not have had roses adorned at our feet or bands blaring at our entrance, but one thing is for sure—and that is you will hear the last trumpet sound and the dead in Christ will rise and the party will be non-stop. I don't know about all the hell you've been going through, but it was for a purpose. Keep pushing, keep praying and adorn yourself with the oil of joy and watch God work.

He said, in Proverbs 17:22, "***a joyful heart is good medicine***." We could all use a little joy. Right? So remember when you're going through your peaks and valleys, God wants you to always guard your heart. It's time for your ordination. Let Jesus handle your breakthrough!

It's Restoration Time

Have you ever driven your car and noticed the wheels were out of balance? You know how it is—you're driving along and you take your hand off the steering wheel and it veers to the right or left. That is how it is in life. When we are off balance we tend to only go in one direction. We need to apply that old nursery song from the movie, **"Jungle Book."** We need to apply the "bear necessities." We need to accentuate the positive and eliminate the negative. In other words, we need to exceed the time we spend praising and building up one another than we do tearing down one another. You know the bible states in Proverbs 14:1, *"the wise woman builds her house, but a fool tears it down with her own hands."* If you don't like that one, I have another one for you. Psalms 127:1 states, *"unless the Lord builds the house; it's builders labor in vain."* Another way of saying it is if we don't have Christ in us; working through and with us we are spinning our wheels and going in one direction. And it is the wrong way.

We need to be about our father's business. You do know he is coming soon. And I'm sure none of us want to be caught with our work undone. We all have some work to do. We might as well get busy doing it because my bible tells me "night cometh and no man can work." We should all be actively employing the ministry of reconciliation. Reconciling is two parties agreeing to go in the same direction. If you haven't endured what Christ or Paul did then you have no reason not to reconcile with your family member or friend. Look at:

- Esau and Jacob

- Joseph and his brothers

- Hosea and Gomer

- Euodia and Syntyche

- Jesus and the world

Jacob tricked his brother Esau into selling his birthright. But in the end the two reconciled. Joseph taunted his brothers because he was a visionary and they were not. But in the end the brothers reconciled. Hosea married a former prostitute and yet he was able to reconcile with her even after she had cheated on him. Euodia and Syntyche were two women leaders in the church who had a falling out, but in the end they were able to reconcile. And lest we forget the greatest example of all time—is Jesus Christ. He forgave. And He reconciled the world to himself. Who are we that we can't model our forefathers and foremothers in the bible? The way we should look at ourselves is the way God looks at us. We should not look through the lens of condemnation; ridicule or backbiting; but rather persevere through affliction—because 1 Peter 3:9 says, *"because of this you were called so that you can inherit a blessing."* We are to *"not repay evil with evil or insult with insult, but give a blessing."* The bible states, *"God is our refuge and strength, and ever present help in trouble."* (Psalm 46:1).

There are some of us here who relish nursing our sores; our scars, our wounds, rather than letting the Word of God; the balm of Gilead, the salve of the Holy Spirit to soothe our pain. We must remember God is the Chief Architect. We are laborers and his fellow ambassadors commissioned to carry out his work and build his kingdom for his glory; not our own! We are builders. We are soldiers in God's army. We need to be working for the King of Kings.

Our work is a privilege. It is a birthright of entitlement. Our work is propelling us closer to our prize. Our work is purposeful. It is for God's Glory! Our work is praise-worthy!

When you find yourself going off in the wrong direction you need to check your alignment. See if you need a front-end alignment. Chances are you haven't been spending much time in God's Word. Chances are you haven't been helping someone in need. Chances are you haven't been hiding God's Word in your heart. You can get a front—end alignment by putting God FIRST at the beginning of your day. You can get a front-end alignment by dropping to your knees and allowing the Holy Spirit to direct your path. You can get a front-end alignment by staying the course and creating a better world for those around you. We must work the work of the One who sent us while it is day because night comes and no man can work. We must do the work of the father. He is our Master. He is our Redeemer. He is our Heavenly Father and the Righteous Judge. We need him to help us in time of need.

James 1:22 says, ***"be doers of the word; not hearers only."*** As Christians we should doers, not just hear what we ought to do, but be about it. Consider your final destination. Your final destination is in Heaven. You're going to take your character with you into Heaven—not your possessions, problems or your pain. It is the relationships you will remember when you leave this place. Therefore, it is important that you get your heart right. Get your attitude right. And get your personality right with your family today. Whatever you have been harboring; whether it is ill-will; resentment or unforgiveness it's time to squash it and let it go. We are all connected through our Heavenly Father. So, let's keep the faith and run the race. With Heaven as our goal and final resting place it behooves us to do it. Remember our work here is:

- A Priviledge;
- Propelling us to the Prize;
- Purposeful and
- Praise-worthy

It's time for restoration. God will show up and show out. We merely need to allow him to manifest his timing. And watch for his results. Are you ready to be restored?

It's Time to Fight!

In life, I believe we have many bouts. But there are three that are noteworthy. First, we fight with people; secondly, we fight with the establishment (i.e., status quo, society, etc.,); and thirdly, we fight with ourselves. We seem to be constantly going in and out of bouts. We all have a little fight in us—otherwise I don't think we would be here if we didn't. Our ancestors had to fight to survive. And I believe they passed that survival instinct on to us.

Now why is it that we fight with people? I believe it is because we are programmed to do so. Remember Eve in the Garden of Eden? She fought against her purpose because she was deceived. You're probably fighting with others too—because you don't know your purpose. But you can, if you ask God and seek him with a sincere heart.

Why do we fight with the establishment? I believe it is because we want equity. We want equal opportunity and equal access. Our fight against the establishment stems from institutionalized racism. We refuse to be disrespected, discarded and disenfranchised. That's why we must fight when it is right. The fight is right when it is for the good of your race, your spiritual convictions or your ethics.

Thirdly, I believe we fight ourselves because we like Eve have been deceived. Now it's time to fight for what's rightfully yours. God said, in his word, "*fight the good fight of faith*." (1 Tim 6:12). When you do that he will guide you. And no matter how life tries to knock you down—you can stand because God's word says, "*he will never let the righteous fall.*" (Psalm 55:22). It just won't work! It's time to fight for what is right.

So when you find yourself up against the ropes and trouble is moving in all around you—all you have to do is 1) save your strength; 2) start soaking in his presence; and 3) saturate your mind with the Word. God has your back! You may have been wronged by another person, but don't sweat it. Instead of vehemently espousing the injustices inflicted upon you, stop reliving it. Save your strength by soaking in His presence. You can soak in God's presence by spending quality time alone in a quiet place. You can soak in God's presence by allowing the noisy rushing waters of ineptness to be silenced by the rivers of living water.

Soaking will suffocate the insignificance of complacency and drown out the dismal dread of despair. If you soak and float in His presence God says, "*when you pass through the waters I will be with you; when you pass through the rivers, they will not sweep over you . . . I am the Lord Your God, the Holy One of Israel, Your Savior.*" (Psalm 43:3). Soaking and floating in His presence is simply keeping your mind on His Word by reading it day and night. When you do that then you can finish the fight; stay on course and save your strength because God is your Lord of Lords. He is the King of Kings. You don't have to fight because His purposes will stand. He knows the beginning and what is still to come. (Isaiah 46:9-11). So remember, what he said, "*I will strengthen you and help you, I will uphold you with my righteous right hand.*" (Isaiah 41:10). There is no doubt God will definitely bring you out as a winner when you trust him.

So the next time the enemy tries to take a punch at you—veer to the right and simply say, "*I am not afraid or discouraged because of this vast army. For the battle is not mine; it is the Lord's.*" (2 Chronicles 10:15b). When life strikes you with bouts of depression, anger, hostility, unforgiveness, sexual promiscuity; financial trouble or overeating; fight back with, "*God is my refuge and my fortress, my God in whom I trust.*" (Psalm 92:1). Remember God has covered you. He will lead you to victory and never defeat. Psalm 92:7-8, states, "*a thousand may fall at your side, ten thousand at your right hand, but it will not come near you. You will only observe with your eyes and see the punishment of the wicked.*" HALLELUJAH! God will not let any harm come to you. And he will allow you to see the enemy fall. Praise God! He is amazing! Remember the words of the prophet Moses in Exodus 14:13, when he said, "*do not be afraid, stand still and you will see the deliverance the Lord will bring you today.*" You can fight or you can yield to His will. What will it be?

Living Out Your Purpose

God intends for you to be more than what you can see. We need to look at ourselves through the eyes of God and discover our potential. Is that's hard for you to phantom? If so, pretend you're a child—full of imagination and wonder. Remember? Now with that same kind of child-like innocence and curiosity transport yourself to your life's dream. Imagine doing that thing or things you saw yourself doing when you were care-free; free from worrying about money, bills, life, shelter, food etc. God gave you a vision of "who" you are in HIM a long time ago. You need to embrace that picture, expect it and be exuberant about seeing it to fruition. It's your dream. The bible states, "**where there is no revelation (vision) the people cast off restraint**." (Proverbs 28:18a). In other words, the people perish.

I believe we need to keep a visual image of our dreams in our mind and in our physical surroundings. It will catapult you beyond your wildest aspirations. Many of us work for a living and have major responsibilities to uphold. But you must see yourself beyond working for a living. Your body make-up is multi-faceted, multi-dimensional and multi-complex. You are capable of achieving so much more than just being a mother, a wife, a husband, etc. Your life in Jesus is still a mystery until you embark on your adventure that will transform you into eternity.

I believe we should speak positive proclamations to ourselves daily. This will motivate and inspire you to be your best. For instance say, **"I am not an accident. I am a perfect design. I am**

God's creation. His plan for me is perfect. I am valuable. God is using me in a powerful way." These life-changing proclamations will infuse and inspire you to work harder and be better. The word of God states, *"the tongue has the power of life and death and those who love it will eat its fruit."* (Proverbs 18:21). Choose to speak positive words of affirmation about your life.

I am excited about living out my life's purpose. I know there is more to me than being a community liaison for the Austin Police Department. I was created for greatness. I know it. And you should know that you are too. Start speaking it and then you will begin to believe it. Seeing your dreams manifest will not be far away. In Psalm 139:16, it states, *"Your eyes saw my substance, being yet unformed. And in your book they are all were written the days fashioned for me when as yet there was none of them."* In other words, God saw you before you were born and he knew what you were going to look like. He knew how long you would be on this earth and when He would transport you to eternity. He knew all this before you came into existence. Our all-knowing, all-wise God knows all the intricate details of our life. Why are we trying to figure it out and not just living life on purpose? We need to be about our Father's business. For some of us that means starting our own business; creating multiple streams of income; writing our books; finishing school or discarding some destructive habits out of our life. Whatever that it is—you need to get busy today. Don't wait. Tomorrow is too late. Do it now.

Jeremiah 29:11 states, *"I know the plans I have for you . . . plans to prosper you and give you a future."* God wants you to be blessed, prosperous and joyful. You were created to be a blessing so that you can bless others. Stop procrastinating, stop using excuses. Start seeding into your potential by placing things or people in your path that will germinate and blossom into your success. Always begin and end with the Word of God. It is still the number one book of all times. Where else is there a better plan for your life's purpose?

Loyalty

What is loyalty? It is faithful duty to a person, place or thing. Duty implies obligation. A person has an obligation to themselves; their family, spouse, job the government and God. You are obligated to take care of yourself. You are obligated to be devoted to your spouse. You are obligated to work. You are obligated to pay your taxes to the government. And finally, you are obligated to serve God if you are a Christian. Since our most supreme and important relationship is to God; it is therefore conceivable to deduce that one's chief's obligation should be to God. Hopefully we are obligated to God, our spouse, or job and to our family.

But why should we be loyal? We should be loyal to God because Jesus promises us more blessings. In the parable of the talents (Matt 25:14-21) Jesus gives an illustration of a owner giving his servants several talents and then he leaves to go on a trip. When he returns the servant with the five talents gives his boss five more. The owner responds to the servant by stating, "well done good and faithful servant; you have been faithful with a little. I will put you in charge of more." In other words, the owner commends his servant for being loyal. And it is the same with God. He knows when you have done the right thing with a little and he will reward us with more. When we have proven we are trustworthy God will grant us more blessings.

Another word for loyalty is faithful. In the parable of the talents the servant showed that he was faithful. And as a result he was rewarded. Can you be faithful when things don't go your way? It's easy to be loyal when things are going well, but what happens when things go awry? When things go wrong at work, at home; in the church; what do you do? When things go wrong in your relationships—do you start wavering on your loyalty? What happens to your loyalty when you don't get what you desire?

Our focal passage is in Luke 12:11, but before we go there, let's read the previous verses in Luke 12:1-11. Jesus said be on your guard against the yeast of the Pharisees. Yeast symbolized evil doctrine, corruption, malice and disintegration. Another way of putting it is that "yeast" symbolized the "energy of sin." In the Old Testament it was against the Mosaic law to use yeast when presenting an offering to God except on two occasions; those two occasions were the grain and the peace offering (Leviticus 23:11; Leviticus 7:13).

In verse one Jesus warns his disciples not to be people pleasers. He tells them don't avoid trouble by trying to please the Scribes and the Pharisees. The Pharisees were notorious for not following their own laws. I know that sounds a lot like some preachers. But aren't we guilty too? That is what you called hypocrisy. It seems difficult at times not being a people pleaser. After all we want people to like us; and it seems easy to "*act the part*" that we want others to see, but at what expense? As men and women of God we have to determine in our minds, either we are going to be loyal or we're going to be a hypocrite. Which would you rather be called a hypocrite or a faithful servant?

The greek word for yeast is "zume." It means "one who plays a part." Modern day times are no different than Old Testament when it comes to hypocrisy. There are hypocrites in every walk of life. Hypocrites are people who try to impress others in order to hide their real selves. In the Christian life, a hypocrite is someone who tries to appear more spiritual than he or she really is. These people know they are pretending and they hope that they will not be found out. Their Christian life is only a shallow masquerade. Is that you?

Somebody is asking why is she talking about hypocrites? The reason is because it is the opposite of loyalty. I submit to you today the best way to ward off hypocrisy is to be loyal! So how can we keep hypocrisy out of our lives? I say we should remember one of God's greatest commandments . . . . "to love the Lord God with all of our heart, mind and soul." That is loyalty! And there will be evidence in your fruit!

But here Jesus warns his disciples not to be like the Pharisees. The Pharisees don't practice what they preach. Sound familiar? Jesus compares hypocrisy to yeast—something every Jew associates with evil. Like yeast hypocrisy starts small but grows quickly and quietly. As it grows it infects the whole person. Hypocrisy does the same thing. Hypocrisy does to the ego what yeast does to bread dough. It puffs it up. Soon pride takes over and a person's character deteriorates quickly. Just like yeast swells up bread; sin can infiltrate our hearts and shrink our character.

If we want to keep hypocrisy out of our lives we must avoid that first bite of yeast. Once we start to pretend the process of hypocrisy accelerates quickly and we no longer act or look the same. We become pretenders, perpetrators, and puppets. The more hypocrisy goes unchecked, the worst it gets. Sir Walter Scott wrote: "oh what a tangled web we weave when we practice to deceive."

Jesus warns his disciples against hypocrisy because eventually it will be discovered. (Read Luke 2:2-3). In other words, your shaking and faking will be revealed for the fraud you are if you keep on doing deceitful things. Jesus goes on to say in verse 4 why should you be afraid of people who can kill the body. He said you should rather, "fear the one who after the body is dead; can throw you into hell." That's who you should fear. He is the Son of Man.

In verse 7 Jesus tells his disciples how much God cares about them. He tells them he loves them so much that he knows the amount of hairs on their heads. That is intimacy. He compares you to sparrows and tells us that we are more important than them. If he knows how many hairs on our head, surely he knows you better than you know yourself. So who do you think you're fooling? You might fool some of the people some of the time; but you can never fool God. Loyalty is about your character. Your character is your behavior—it is how you treat others. How do you handle controversial situations? Do you crumble under pressure or do you stand like a rock?

Loyalty is honesty. When it comes to temptation are you loyal to God or to your flesh? For some of us our biggest test of loyalty is in our flesh. And God is saying refuse to succumb to your senses instead submit to the Spirit. Then you will NOT sink to your flesh.

Are you reliable and consistent when it comes to exercising God's Word? Are you a wishy washy Christian who just plays a part? The bible states, "bad company corrupts good character." So even if you are a good Christian if you constantly associate with people of unsavory character it will affect you adversely.

What about how you deal with money? Do you demonstrate loyalty and obligation to God in that area? The bible states, *"if you are dishonest with a little you are going to be dishonest with a lot."* (Luke 16:10). So who are you when nobody is looking?

Some of us have not been loyal to God. We play church. We practice religion. But we don't have a real relationship with the Father. Our loyalty has diminished. It's gone limp. Our allegiance to God is weak, shaky and down-right disgraceful. And some of us don't show loyalty to leadership. God is calling someone in here to give proper respect to your leaders. The bible states, *"obey your leaders and submit to their authority . . . obey them so that their work will be a joy, not a burden for that would be no advantage to you."* (Hebrews 13:7,17). Are you obligated to God when it's time for prayer meeting? Sunday School? Mission and Outreach or do you make excuses for your devotion to God?

Some of us are more loyal to our jobs, our schools, our churches rather than the people we are in relationship with. Why is that?

Hypocrisy is one of the worst enemies for a Christian. Why is that? I believe it is because hypocrisy breeds complacency and mediocrity. It is foolish and futile. It doesn't evoke change. And if we're not carful that complacency will creep up in the church until you have a dead church with dead people disintegrating to the grave with no one with a shovel to dig them out.

Can I paint you a picture of loyalty? Go to 1 Chronicles 28:9-10. David is a great example of loyalty. Solomon had been chosen to build the Temple as a Sanctuary for the Ark of the Covenant. But David charges his son; Solomon to complete the work. He showed his allegiance and faithfulness in small matters and God elevated him to rule over much. As a young boy David was a faithful shepherd boy tending sheep. He was a faithful hunter killing lions, tigers and bears. And as a young man he was faithful to his family by slaying the Giant Goliath. David was loyal to his call. He was an accomplished musician; a loyal hunter, shepherd and warrior. God crowned David King of Israel and he reigned for 40 years. That was his reward for loyalty. He lived a good long life, and he was wealthy and highly respected. Hs son, Solomon succeeded him and carried on his legacy. As a result he too was blessed abundantly.

In the 29th chapter of 1 Chronicles David offers a prayer to God. In verse 16 he concludes his prayer by reaffirming his request for God to keep the people's heart loyal to him. What is the lesson for us? We must not forget how good God has been when we are NOT struggling. Lest we forget to quick— we must keep ourselves in constant conflict with our flesh so that we don't get so puffed up and lose sight of our purpose. God wants his people faithful to him. No substitution will do.

No imitation will do. True loyalty comes from true devotion. Devotion is uncompromising obedience to the Father, no matter what. If you are going to be loyal, I believe we should possess these three traits. We should be:

- teachable (moldable to accept correction and instruction)

- humble (admit when you don't know it all; and vulnerable)

- honest (unwavering, with unbroken integrity)

We must be like flint; hard as nails and tough as rubber. We must remember God cannot be punked! He cannot be pimped nor can he be prostituted! If you're going to be loyal you must examine your character. Look in the mirror and ask God who you are. Ask him what part of your character do I need to work on? If you keep living and doing what God told you to do; sooner or later someone is going to bring a charge against you. My question is how will you respond?

Luke 21:15 says, **"make up your mind not to worry beforehand how you will defend yourselves, for I will give you words and wisdom that none of your adversaries will be able to resist or contradict."** In other words, we must learn from our past failures to understand what didn't work before. It is in that condition that you have a teachable moment. You have to make a decision, either' I'm going to learn from my past failures, mistakes and disappointment or I am going to keep walking down the same old path? I believe there are two ways to learn:

- Crash and burn or

- Listen and learn

If you choose to speak your mind then consequently you'll probably fall in the crash and burn category. But if you choose to listen and learn the Holy Spirit will teach you what to do and what to say. So when your co-workers, your boss, church folk or your spouse accuses you of wrong doing that's when you call on the Holy Spirit to step in. He will give you what to say. If you're loyal to him—he will show up on your behalf. If you are willing to align yourself up with his Word, Will and Way, God will be compelled to act. The bible states, "he won't withhold any good thing from you." That's when the Holy Spirit will step in and give you the words of wisdom to say. As a result those duplicitous detractors of the law and mutilators of the flesh will scurry in shame. Why? They will scurry because your bear your father's name.

Jesus in his humanity could have struck back at the Pharisees and Sadducees for calling him a demon and blasphemer, but he didn't (Luke 22:65). Instead he got them told in the most Christian way. His words were immutable. His words could not be repudiated or annulled. The 21st chapter of Luke is a great example of Jesus exerting his authority. He doesn't have to defend his word. He is the Word. And he is the only divine authority on the subject. Once the Holy Spirit steps on the scene all scoffers are silenced. Wouldn't you want to have him on your side in an argument, in a battle or in life? So why don't we heed his word? Let's practice loyalty and begin today. What about it? You can choose hypocrisy or loyalty. What will it be?

Out of the Box

What have you been doing? Is there something on your mind that won't go away? God says whatever your heart is there is where your treasure is. (Luke 12:34). There have been many people to discover that what God wants is obedience. Myself included. My question is what are you spending your time on?

In life, we may find that our biggest enemy is not the devil, but rather ourselves. We venture through life with baggage and preconceived notions on how we think things ought to go; not realizing God has a bigger plan; a bigger vision and the best resources to get it done. What am I saying? I am saying that for far too long many of us have been suffering from a case of paralysis. We suffer from "paralysis through analysis." We think too much about *"what if"* rather than walking by faith and doing what we believe God is calling us to do.

Some of us have this mind-set when it comes to worship. We have pre-scripted praise songs, pre-scripted prayers and pre-scripted rituals we do Sunday after Sunday. We need to throw away that "traditionalist" viewpoint when it comes to worshiping God. How about if you praise God outside the box and watch what happens. The bible says, "***true worshipers, "worship God in spirit and in truth.***" (John 4:24). If that is the truth why aren't you doing it? Your worship experience with God may cause you to lift holy hands in the sanctuary. It may cause you to stomp your feet or dance. Whatever you are led by the Spirit of God to do; that is what you should do.

For many years I have been in a Baptist Church. I've witnessed countless praise and worship services. But there have not been many Baptist churches that I have encountered where I witnessed the Holy Spirit freely moving in the sanctuary. What I mean is that I have not seen the type of freedom in worship where church-goers were uninhibited. I know for a fact that if someone were to speak in an unknown tongue during Sunday morning worship the saints would look at that person with disdain. If the Spirit of God moved a worshiper to dance and run around the church; I am a positive there would be scoffers shaking their heads in objection. And if a worshiper was led by the Spirit of God to stand on their feet and worship God throughout the service; I am sure someone would be appalled. What is that about? Who appointed us judge? We have no business trying to dictate or relegate what worship should look like. Our responsibility and commandment is to worship God in spirit and in truth. We, as children of God, should be free to do that without fear, backlash or scorn. It doesn't matter what that looks like. As long as you're worshiping God with a sincere heart, that is freedom, not fear. The bible says, "**whom the Son sets free is free indeed.**" (John 8:36). If we are free then our worship experience should reflect his glory in whatever expression that looks like.

Corinthians 3:17, states, "**where the Spirit of the Lord is; there is freedom.**" If the Spirit of the Lord is reigning in your church; there should be some evidence of his presence. Freedom is devoid of barriers. Freedom is activity not complacency. It is a spirit of joy and liberality. It is a personal sense of self-expression without ridicule or judgment.

God's Spirit evokes the gifts of the Spirit. Those gifts are outlined in 1 Corinthians 12 and moreover in Galatians 5:22-26. We need to come out of the box and give God the praise for all he has done, will do and is doing. Are there any true worshipers in the house? If they are you need to come out of the box. I mean really come out of the box. Once you're out; stay out of the box. Don't come out one Sunday and then go back in the box next Sunday. God is not limited by man's regulations and rules. But he gives the ***"Spirit without limit."*** (John 3:34). For me that means God is omniscient and has all the power to do whatever he pleases. It's not about what pleases you, but it's about what pleases him. What pleases God is what he said in 1 Samuel 15:22, ***"to obey rather than sacrifice."*** And the thing that God requires is to ***"act justly, love mercy and walk humbly with Him."*** (Micah 6:8). As true worshipers of God we need to walk according to his way and give him the praise that is due his name. Will you come out of the box?

Peace of God

Philippians 4:4-7

Paul speaks to the Philippian church about the "peace of God." This peace we cannot fathom with our natural mind. We need God to give it. The jaws of anxiety grip us with an unrelenting choke hold. We try to muster up the strength to break free, but to no avail. Tension, stress, uneasiness is ever present. What do we do? Paul says ask, pray, petition and with thanksgiving.

The gift of peace is not automatic. You can't will it, wish it, or blink it into being. Paul says we must ask! What happens when we ask? Paul says the "peace of God that transcends all understanding will guard your heart and mind." Let's break that down. Peace of God; it is not the peace of world, it is not the peace of Harry Krishner; it is not the peace of Allah, but it is the peace of God—we don't know what that is until we experience it.

Then Paul says that transcends our understanding. What does transcend mean? It means to o beyond what I can conceive, imagine or think. It goes beyond my comprehension, my knowledge and my ability to cope or reason. It is aloof, it is allusive, it is beyond my reach. That is why I can't get it unless I ask God for it. I have to ask God because it originates with God. It is not external. It is not in the cosmos, it is not in the natural. Rather it is the supernatural, incomprehensible, mystery of God! I want it. I need it, but I can't receive it until

I ask God for it. I believe you want it too. Let me tell you what happens when you get it.

Paul says when God gives it to you—God will shield your heart and your mind in him. In other words, when the reality of your situation has you perplexed, messed up, shut up from the world and your despair looms over your head like a thunderous cloud, your reality tells you there is no way of this mess. The doctor says there is no hope; there is no food in the cupboard; and your child is hungry. What do you do?

Paul says God will invade your reality with his peace. He will give you peace in the middle of the storm. He will break loose a banner and declare war on the enemy. The flu epidemic can break out and your child can be in prison, but God will keep your mind. It may feel like you're ready to snap, crack and pop; but God. Trouble may be closing in on you from every side, but God will sustain your brain and prevent you from going crazy. The world can deliver you the toughest blow to challenge your reasoning and rational thinking, but God will say, "No, not my child." You see God will keep you from creeping into insanity with his Word. God will keep you from snatching a hole in someone flesh because of the witness of your own testimony. God will keep your mind in perfect peace if you truly rely on him.

Paul says he will keep your heart in peace. That tells me that God will overshadow the mayhem and provide peace. He will keep my mind from snapping and being sent to an insane asylum. He will keep my mind from twisting and emptying a pistol in someone's head. He will keep me from destroying my body when I want to give up. He will lift up a standard and prevent harm from coming near my mind. Nothing can penetrate the force field of God's peace. God's peace is beyond what I can explain. It is infinite. It supercedes logic. It goes beyond my imagination. It far exceeds my intellect. It baffles the wise. It confounds comprehension. It just doesn't make sense to the natural man.

The peace that God gives resides in a place of utter paradise. It is hidden away from the cacophony of chaos. It nestled within a realm of solitude. It is tucked between the corners and crevices of God's mind. It is in his holy presence. God's peace transcends all reality. God's peace catapults your mind into a symphony of solace. It is unmistakably quiet, comfortable and refreshing. God's peace shines in darkness. God's peace stands when things fall. God's peace builds and never destroys. God's peace strengthens in weakness. God's peace positions you for greatness. And God's peace sustains sinners. It is a perpetual fountain of rejuvenation. It's recharging and refilling constantly.

And then Paul says he will keep your heart. In other words, Paul is saying God will guard your heart. Your heart is the core of your character. It is with the heart we accept Christ. It is with the heart that we believe and trust God. It is with the heart that opens you up to the relationship with God and man. Yeah, God will shut down, annihilate and destroy anything that tries to attack your heart when you are in the throes of anxiety. Even our ambassadors of faith can testify to God's ability to guard our heart.

Look at Daniel in the Lion's den. He was thrown into a cave with ravenous lions, but because he prayed to God he closed the mouth of the lions. And Daniel experienced perfect peace. How many of us can say that we have the peace of God? If you want to experience the peace of God you have to ask. You have to believe he will give it.

Another example of God' guarding your heart is when Paul was on his second missionary journey. He was in a Roman prison, chained to one guard and serving as King Nero's prisoner. Paul was known for preaching the Old Testament. The guards were non-believers and they had never heard the Word. Paul began preaching and the prison guards heard the Word being preached. As a result they were converted. It didn't bother Paul that his enemy was keeping him captive. He continued to preach. His heart didn't prevent him for witnessing. God guarded Paul's heart even as a prisoner. He can do the same for you. It doesn't matter what your position. What matters is the position of your heart. Paul's heart was near and dear to God. Because Paul's heart was dedicated to pleasing and honoring God; God guarded his heart. Once Paul was converted he was sold out for Christ. He didn't allow any man or woman to sway his convictions. While preaching the Word of God, Paul led Lydia and Philip to Christ and they were converted (Acts 16:14-34). God demonstrated to Paul that he will guard your heart. Therefore, we can experience God's peace when we ask him.

It is common to assumption that we should praise him with thanksgiving when we ask. The real test of guaranteeing God's peace is to believe that you will receive it when you ask. God never lies. He never forgets about you or leaves you hanging. He can be trusted. And his Word cannot be impeached. Philippians 4:11 states, ***"the peace of God will guard your heart and mind***

in Christ Jesus." God's Word cannot be vetoed, revoked or rescinded therefore we as Christians should wield the power of the Word with careful precision and responsibility. Simply put, we should expect it to fulfill the purpose that God intended. You can have peace and protection when you place your heart in the Master's hand.

Reconciling Our Relationships

What is God saying to you about your relationship with people? How do you treat your family, friends and associates? More importantly, how do you treat God? The purpose for these questions is to get to the root of the problem. Self. Many times we do not acknowledge the fact that we have pent up anger or unresolved issues with our immediate family or spouse. We tend to minimize our weaknesses and enumerate the other person's faults; when all we're doing is avoiding our own. The reality is we need to face our own inadequacies.

In the past several months I believe God is speaking to his people about our relationships. In my own life God is saying specifically, "I have given you time to reflect, refrain and recapture." In other words, he is saying that he has given me time to reflect on how good he has been in the past, refrain from being so busy doing stuff in the present; and recapture the essence of who I am. By doing so, then I can focus on his purpose for me in the future. Wow! How poignant and powerful.

Again, we can see the root of the problem. It is self. I believe God is saying the same to all of us. We need to be more focused on the things he deems important, not on what we think is important. We know from the Word of God that people are important to God. His Word says, *"My dwelling place will be with them; I will be their God, and they will be my people."* (Ezekiel 37: 27). That is why we need to revive, reconcile or rekindle our relationships with people. God wants us to commune with him constantly. (*John 15:5*). If our horizontal relationship with people isn't right than our vertical relationship with God surely won't be either. It's not our career, our fancy car or our home that people will talk about at our funeral, but it is how we treated others. Your relationship with people will follow you into eternity. That is why it is so important for us to treat people right now.

So much has happened to many of us in the past year. And now here we are in a new year. We're embarking on a new path. What will that look like? My prayer is that you will embrace what God is showing you about yourself and you will invest time in redefining yourself. By that I mean, take time to reflect in prayer what you have done in your past. Ask God to reveal to you what areas in your life need work. Then get to work doing it. That sounds pretty deep doesn't it? But that is what it will take to get to the root of our problem. When we spend time alone with God in personal meditation, not talking or whining about our problems, but just sitting still and allowing Him to bring things to our remembrance you will discover more about Him and you. Our character is who we are. Until we are ready to face the truth about ourselves we will continue to have psuedo relationships that are superficial and unfulfilling. If you care about yourself and how God sees you it's worth the investment.

There are many ways we can choose to spend our time. But time spent alone with God is never wasted. We have to prioritize our lives. When you put your life in perspective and place the Creator of the Universe first in all you do than your life will work out for your good. Why? Because you have a heavenly viewpoint on what is important. And God says in his Word, **"all**

*things work together for the good, for those who love me (God)
and are called according to my purpose."* (*Romans 8:28*). If you
want your life to work out for your good try placing God first
in all you do. Then expect to see the results of His handiwork
in your life.

In the book of Matthew we read about Simon's relationship
with Jesus. Because Jesus valued his relationship with Simon so
much it says, *"I (Jesus) prayed for you."* (*Luke 22:32*) Can you
imagine? Jesus actually goes before the Father on your behalf
and prayed for your good? That's remarkable! It's incredible!
It's expected when you're in right relationship with your Savior.
He is the Master. He is the King. He is Ruler of everything! He
always has your best interest at heart. That verse alone should
motivate you to rush and reconcile any unresolved qualm you
have with a family member, friend or co-worker. The bible
tells us when we forgive God hears and answers our prayers.
(*Mark 11:25*). We need only to activate our faith and follow this
command. We should love our neighbor as we love our self.
(*Matt 22:39*). When we act on the Word of God by applying
it in our everyday life then we possess power to conquer any
and all things. What does your relationship with Jesus look like?

The Lord is Good

How do you taste the Lord? You can taste and see God is good because he told us that He is our daily bread. When you have nothing else to eat; try feasting on the Word of God. We can taste and see the Lord is good by taking him at His Word. Whenever you have a problem go to God so that He can solve it. If you're faced with fear go to God's Word in 1 Tim 1:7 where it says, **"God didn't give us a Spirit of fear, but of love, power and a sound mind."** If you're mind is confused and you don't know what to do check out Paul's letter to the Philippians in 4:8, where he says, **"think on these things, whatsoever is lovely, whatsoever is pure, whatsoever is a good report think on these things."**

You know that you can taste and see that the Lord is good because his word is inspired straight from the throne of God. In Ephesians 5:2, God says, **"he hath given himself for us an offering and a sacrifice to God for a sweet smelling savor."** His word tells us that his ordinances are sure and altogether righteous. They are more precious than gold, than much pure gold; they are sweeter than honey, than honey from the comb. (Psalm 19:10). Can you taste him? All you need is the Lord. He will make your life sweet. He will give you plenty to eat. You know the Lord is good because he has not changed. Remember when you where young and didn't do everything right, but God had mercy on you. Now that you're older the bible tells you in Psalm 37:25, **"now I'm old, but I never seen the righteous forsaken or his seed begging bread."**

You can taste and see the Lord is good because when you were sick and needed to get well God was there. Remember what he said in Jeremiah 8:22, "is there a balm in Gilead?" He told us in Isaiah 53:5 that he was, *"pierced for our transgressions. He was crushed for our iniquities, the punishment that brought us peace was upon him and by his stripes (wounds) we are healed."* God did all of that so that we can walk in newness of life. He didn't do it so that we can be depressed or be in physical ailment, but He did it so that we can live fortified and productive lives. Peter said Christ bore all sin in his body. He bore all sickness and diseases on the Cross, so that we will have the right for eternal life. Oh taste and see the Lord is good. Can't you just savor his goodness? He told us, *"many are the afflictions of the righteous—but the Lord deliver us out of those troubles."* (Psalm 37:4).

Psalm 43:19 says, *"see I am doing a new thing! Now it springs up; do you not perceive it? I am making a way in the desert and streams in the wasteland."* God is doing a new thing your life. What new things is God doing? It's there. Are you paying attention? You see it's Satan's job to distract us from our divine assignment. The enemy will keep you busy being busy so that you lose sight of what God is doing or showing you. Can I help you with something? In my own life I've been so busy— busy doing good work—church work—ministry work—all for the Lord—but I wasn't paying attention to God's voice—telling me what He wanted me to do. Have you ever found yourself being that way? For example, I was 2nd vice president of Church Women United; I mentored women recently released from prison; I performed as Decorations Chair and Ice Breaker

Mistress of Ceremony in the Metamorphosis Ministry; I held the Recording Secretary position in Agape Minister's Wives Auxiliary; I was a member of the Baptist Minister's Wives Auxiliary & Vicinity; I was a Sunday School Teacher at my local church and I was the Women's Ministry Teacher and the Special Events Coordinator; and I was a member of the African American Chamber of Commerce and finally I started my own public speaking business. Now how many of you out there know that's too busy? You see I didn't even mention my job, my family or my husband did I? The laundry list of busyness will keep you in the throes of stress and confusion. It's not the place God designed for you. Yeah, he wants to perform a new thing in your life, but if you're not paying attention long enough to hear His voice how can you perceive or discern it?

God wants you to taste and he wants you to see that he is good. He knows you have a mouth because he hears your cries for mercy and grace. He knows you have eyes because He gave you eyes to see His goodness in your life. Now it's time for you to trust him with your divine assignment. He chose you. Let him use you. Your divine destiny is in his hands. Your heart is in his Hands. Isaiah 40:29-3 says, **"he gives strength to the weary and increase the power to the weak. Even youths grow tired and weary, and young men stumble and fall; but those who hope in the Lord will renew their strength. They will soar on wings like eagles, they will run and not grow weary, they will walk and not faint."** You see God will keep you.

He will keep you from losing your mind. He will keep you from cursing out your co-worker. He will keep you when you're ready to throw in the towel. He will keep you because Isaiah

26:3 states, (HE) *will keep in perfect peace him whose mind is steadfast, because he trusts in you. Trust in the Lord forever, for the Lord, the Lord, is the Rock eternal.*" Being kept by God is like having an umbrella in the middle of the ocean—he will flood you with His love; Being kept by God is like being a baby in a drawer—he will cover you. Being kept by God is like being in a field of flowers—He will fumigate you with his presence.

My Lord is trustworthy if only we would take Him at his word. He said in Proverbs 3:5, "trust in the Lord with all your heart and lean not on your own understanding; in all your ways acknowledge him, and He will make your paths straight." *God is trustworthy.* He can do what no other can do. He is worthy of our praise. He is worthy of our trust. Have you ever been in a situation that you didn't know how it was going to turn out and then all of sudden things got better? It wasn't you. It was God leading you through. We have to trust God in the good times and in the bad times. We have to trust Him with our lives. He said he would never leave or forsake us. We should depend on him for everything in life. The Word says, "be yet not unwise, but understanding what the will of the Lord is." (Eph 5:17). When you understand that you can trust God—He will keep you. Then you can comprehend what the Psalmist meant when he wrote, **"oh taste and see that the Lord is good; blessed is he who trust in him."** (Psalm 34:8).

Weigh Your Words

In recent months, God has shown me that I need to weigh my words more carefully. What I believe he has been showing me is how I speak to others, particularly my husband. (former). I don't know about you, but sometimes I can be mean. You may not have that problem, but I did. I have to be honest; sometimes I still struggle with that. However I'm a work in progress, as we all are. So let's just admit we can use some work weighing our words. I know the bible tells us to speak to each in love. But it's hard to do all the time. Right . . . particularly, if you're operating in the flesh. I know a lot of you are saying, "child, I just can't help myself—that's just how I am." Well, you're wrong. That's right, I said it. You're wrong. The bible states, "*let the word of Christ dwell in you richly as you teach and admonish one another with all wisdom, as you sing psalms, hymns and spiritual songs with gratitude in your hearts to God.*" (Colossians 3:16). That means we should speak to each other in love whether we are teaching, talking or telling someone what they did to hurt us. Even when we are correcting someone about their infraction; we need to do that in love. And it's the same way in reverse. In other words, when someone comes to us to share what God has said to them about our behavior, we need to accept that in love.

One day I took time to write down the responses I gave my husband (former). I was floored. It didn't dawn on me until I saw it in print—how much venom and anger was coming from my lips. I was convicted. When I looked down at the paper I realized why he had been so nasty towards me. It was because the majority of the time all he heard was gripes and complaints. My speech was riddled with comments like, "why didn't you do it," "you're always making excuses," "why does it take you so long to do something I ask you?" Rather than being reactive I should have been proactive! I want you to know the moment I changed my outflow from gripes and complaints to words of appreciation, affirmation and encouragement; he changed his attitude towards me. It was beautiful. I admit that I am still learning, but it was a beautiful process to see God's hand at work in the situation. Praise God that he convicted me and showed me what I needed to change. It is a lesson I believe we can all learn from. Will you?

Something else God showed me in weighing my words is that we need to learn to speak life to our situation. No matter what your circumstances; you can speak life to it. Some people have to battle cancer, some battle with finances; some battle with cantankerous bosses; but God says in His Word; **"the tongue has the power of life and death; and those who love it will eat its fruit."** (Proverbs 18:21). Whatever your situation is, God wants you to speak life to it. So when you're faced with a problem put those words into action! Speak life! Your mind may say, "give up, you can't win," but your mouth and Spirit can say, "*I can do all things through Christ who strengthens me.*" (Philippians 4:13). Your body may say, "it doesn't look god," but your mouth and Spirit can say, "*the punishment that brought me peace is upon me and by Christ's wounds I am healed.*" (Isaiah 53:5b). Your boss may say, "you're a reject and a slacker," but your mouth and Spirit can say, "*an* *honest answer is like a kiss on the lips.*" (Proverbs 24:26). In all situations, God wants you to know that he has your back. Even though our flesh is weak, our spirit is always willing to do what God has called us to.

Make sure you weigh your words carefully. And remember you have the power to speak life or death to your situation. Why not choose life? It's really up to you. How do you see yourself? Do you see yourself as a mighty conqueror or a whimpering washout? You determine the fruit you eat—will it be bitter or sweet?

Where is the Unity in our Community?

Disagreement divides. Disagreement disrupts our equilibrium. Disagreement pits us one against the other. It places us in a peculiar predicament, forcing us to have to choose sides. Are you on this side, or will you be on that side—it separates; creating a schism. It keeps us at bay, up in arms, disconnected, incongruent, causing disunity.

Just the other Sunday I was walking down the street; a few blocks from her. And I was accosted by a young White girl. She looked to be in her mid 20s. She screamed insults and derogatory statements at me—shouting, "not in my neighborhood, Nigger, you better take that over there!" What was my crime? We were at odds. She was on one side, I was on the other. You see; my seminarian sisters and brothers . . . disagreement divides. It runs counter with our convictions. I don't know what was going on in my misguided and misinformed White sister's mind, but I bet it was because she disagreed with my presence in this predominately White neighborhood. Yeah it got bad y'all. I even kindled the fire by hurling insults back at her, but that that didn't get us anywhere. We were in disagreement. We were divided.

And I'm sure if you reflect for a moment on your own life—you can honestly say that you have had a disagreement with someone. No matter what we do, inevitably we will find ourselves in disagreement. Whether it is with our spouse on where to vacation or our significant other on where to go to eat, we are going to be in disagreement.

And you and I are not alone in this. Take America for example. She has encountered colossal disagreements. Give ear and hear some of America's disagreements:

- You can't abolish slavery.

- You can't give women the right to vote.

- You can defeat Nazi Germany.

- You can't cure polio.

- You can't allow Black children to go to school with White children.

- You can put a man on the moon.

- You can't pass a Civil Rights Act.

- You can't beat the Russians in hockey.

- You can't help bring down the Berlin Wall.

- You can't elect a Black man President of the United States of America.

No matter what, somebody somewhere will deny us of something and we will have a disagreement. Slaves disagreed with being denied liberty, dignity and humanity and yet they were the very people who laid the bricks and mortar of our nation's White House. Yeah sisters and brothers there are countless examples of disagreement. I am sure my dear sister Denise and Rosie and maybe even you too Dr. Jennifer Lord have heard someone tell you women can't preach. Whether that idiotic statement came from a man or the Church you found yourself in disagreement; divided on the issue; you were in disunity. There is no question in my mind that disagreement divides us.

Even here at Austin Presbyterian Theological Seminary we can find disagreement. The learned professors are positioned as the altruist insiders possessing knowledge and wisdom and we hungry seminarians are the outsiders hoping to become the insiders of God's hidden mysteries. Yeah church disagreement divides. We find ourselves having to take sides. Are we part of the Enlightened group or the Unlightened group? Are we the Have or the Have-Nots? Are we wise or foolish? Can you help me? It appears we are divided. Can anybody tell me where is the Unity in our Community? Turn to your neighbor and ask them, where is it? And yet some of us masquerade around campus deceiving ourselves as if we possess this allusive trait of unity, when the truth be told we are undercover operatives of disunity. We have vividly colored banners on campus espousing we are an "exemplar Christian community." Hmmm. Exemplar in what? We are exemplar in being divided. I ask you again, "where is the unity in our community?" Maybe you can help me find it?

Recently a fellow seminarian was diagnosed with cancer. And there was a concerted effort to show hospitality and community during her crisis. And that is good. But I failed to see that same kind of unity when yours truly was in similar crisis. I am in disagreement with you church—about our so-called "exemplar Christian community." I am part of this community, but yet I feel disconnected, divided, in disagreement. Maybe you feel it too? I don't know about you, but I want to find it. Can you help me? My disagreement stems from the fact that

I have been hospitalized five times, I have undergone three major surgeries, fainted in class on campus and was rushed to the hospital by EMS and yet there was no community coming to my aid. Can somebody tell me where is the unity in our community?

Yeah, today my brothers and sisters I am in disagreement with our state of affairs. We have missed the mark. We have dropped the ball. The truth is we have failed to execute unity.

The problems we have are not in some nebulous vacuum, set in isolation. Oh no. The problem we have here is the same problem the Christians had in the first century. Look at the text in Philippians 4:2, it states, "Euodia and Syntyche were two women in the church that disagreed. They were probably deaconess. This disagreement had the potential to create irrevocable discord and disunity; so much so that Paul addresses them by name. He even enlists the help of an anonymous mediator, he calls the "loyal yokefellow," and Clement to squash the commotion before it erupts into gangrene and destroys the entire church. And why is Paul handling this disagreement and not the Pastor or the deacons? Maybe it was because Paul was well acquainted with disagreement.

Remember the disagreement with Peter? They were divided. And as a result they parted company. We don't even know what these two women were in disagreement about. Two things we do know are they were laborers in the gospel with Paul and their names were written in the book of life. Yes my brothers and sisters the lack of unity is plaguing our world today, just like back then. However, Paul discloses the secret to achieving unity. He says, "rejoice!" And he is very resolute in his exhortation. He says I will say it again, "Rejoice!" Hmm! Hmm! Paul knows something we don't know. He knows disagreement can produce positive change! AHA! Paul says, "don't be anxious about anything." He tells us if we bring our problem, our anxiety, our trouble to God in prayer it will affect our attitude and our actions. He says, "let your gentleness be evident to all. The Lord is near. Present your requests to God."

And here is the key. How do you present your request to God? Paul tells us in verse six, with "prayer and petition and thanksgiving." And the result is peace! Aha again! The reason why Paul could say "rejoice" in all situations is because he knew prayer and praise produces God's peace. I'll say it again. **Prayer and praise produces God's peace.** That tells me whenever I'm faced with a disagreement, distress or any problem I need to take it to God in prayer. My brothers and sisters—I'm here to testify that God's Word is true. I found that out in my own life after being burglarized three times here on campus. I didn't have any peace. But I noticed that when I prayed and praised God—all anxiety, all stress and despair left. Why? It was because I experienced God's peace! Not only does prayer and praise produce God's peace, but it changes your attitude and your action! Yes, it's true. It may not change my situation, but it definitely changed how I viewed my situation.

I believe Church if we pray together corporately, not in isolation and if we praise God together, not in isolation—we could bring unity back to our community.

Can I call on some witnesses who can testify that praise and prayer produce peace? Let me ask Daniel who was caught in the lion's den. It was because he prayed God closed the mouth of the lions. And remember Paul and Silas locked up in jail. They launched a Hallelujah Praise Party and the jail doors flung open! Jonah was shut up in the belly of a large fish, but when he prayed the fish spit him out on dry land! What about those Jericho Walls?—You know they came tumbling down when the people decided to have an outrageous praise party!

Brothers and Sisters we cannot allow Satan to snatch our praise, our prayers or our peace. We have to rejoice! The Lord is near. Don't be anxious about anything, but in everything present your request to God and the peace of God that transcends all understanding will guard your heart and your mind in Christ Jesus. In the Baptist Church they have a song we sing—"this joy that I have the world didn't give it to me; the world can't take it away!" Sisters and brothers—The Joy Jesus gives no one can take away!

What's Missing?

Our lives are bombarded with chaos, destruction and decay. It seems like no one really cares anymore. There is something missing. What's missing? I dare say what's missing from the fabric of our lives is faith!

What's faith? The Apostle Paul wrote faith is, "the substance of things hoped for, the evidence of things not seen." You may not be able to touch it, smell it or taste it; but you know what it is when you see it demonstrated in someone else's life. You may even see it demonstrated in your own life. That's witnessing faith in action.

I'm going to share three examples of faith in action. Then I'm going to tell you how you can have faith. Take the little Engine for example, he had to muster the faith in himself to get over the mountain. The little engine's obstacle was the mountain. And he exercised faith by saying repeatedly, "I think I can, I think I can, I think, I can." That's what faith is. It is thinking you can.

In your own life you need faith to overcome your problem. By speaking self affirmations to yourself; like, "I think I can, I think I can and you did it. That was faith. If a toy engine believed in itself how much more should we have FAITH in ourselves?

Again, I ask you . . . what's missing? I think we could all use some faith today. Another example of faith in action is Lance

Armstrong. Here is a man that overcame testicular cancer after it had spread throughout his body to his lungs and brain. He later had surgery to remove two brain metastases without taking radiation. And you have to ask yourself how did he do it? I submit to you that he did it by faith! Armstrong demonstrated faith in his own ability. Not only did he recover from cancer in 1999, but he went on to win the Tour De France a record seven times between 1999 through 2005 I call that faith!

Finally, the third person that can attest to faith is the greatest person of faith. That is Jesus Christ! Some of you may believe in him. Some of you may not. I am one who does believe. There is no mistaking Jesus Christ is the pinnacle of faith. He demonstrated his faith by being obedient to his Father's will; even though he did nothing wrong. He was mistreated, ridiculed, and hung on a Cross. But his faith never wavered. It didn't stop. He hung, bled and died so that we wouldn't be lost. He is our Savior. He showed us his faith and told us that all we need is faith in him.

The Apostle Matthew said," I tell you the truth, if you faith is as small as a muster seed, you can say to this mountain, move from here to there and it will move. Nothing will be impossible for you." That is what's missing—our heart's desire to have faith. Faith empowers you to do anything and everything no matter how hard it looks. Our good looks, our intellect, our money or our character will not get it for us. We must have faith!

A scholar wrote, "God can take a lowly vessel, Shape it with his mighty hand, Fill it with a matchless treasure, make it serve a purpose grand."

That's what faith can do. Faith makes your life grand. The missing thing you are seeking is faith. The way to get faith is to open up your heart. Open up your mouth and ask God for it and believe that you can. Just like the Little Engine demonstrated his faith by climbing up the mountain you can. And just like Lance Armstrong demonstrated his faith by surviving cancer and winning seven races you can too. Since that time, we know that Lance Armstrong has been dethroned for those accomplishments. However, we can still use him as an example of achieving greatness. We know not to put our faith in man, but in the man who holds manhood in his hand. Jesus Christ invites you to have faith in him. Faith can conquer any obstacle. Faith can transform your life. Faith can make you victorious. Faith can make you triumphant. Faith will silence your enemies and send naysayers scurrying in shame. For you to possess faith you need only to recite to yourself . . . "I think I can. I think I can. I think I can." And like the Little Engine you will be amazed that you can. Faith is the seed that blooms endless possibilities. Why not ask for some today?